Let's Be Kids and Measure Liquids!

Kelly Doudna

Consulting Editors, Diane Craig, M.A./Reading Specialist
and Susan Kosel, M.A. Education

ABDO
Publishing Company

Published by ABDO Publishing Company, 4940 Viking Drive, Edina, Minnesota 55435.

Credits
Edited by: Pam Price
Curriculum Coordinator: Nancy Tuminelly
Cover and Interior Design and Production: Mighty Media
Photo Credits: AbleStock, Brand X Pictures, Kelly Doudna, Photodisc, ShutterStock,
Wewerka Photography

Library of Congress Cataloging-in-Publication Data

Doudna, Kelly, 1963-
   Let's be kids and measure liquids! / Kelly Doudna.
     p. cm. -- (Science made simple)
   ISBN 10 1-59928-610-6 (hardcover)
   ISBN 10 1-59928-611-4 (paperback)

   ISBN 13 978-1-59928-610-5 (hardcover)
   ISBN 13 978-1-59928-611-2 (paperback)
   1. Volume (Cubic content)--Juvenile literature. 2. Weights and measures--Juvenile literature.
   3. Liquids--Juvenile literature. I. Title. II. Series: Science made simple (ABDO Publishing Company)

QC104.D68 2007
530.8--dc22   2006015228

SandCastle Level: Fluent

SandCastle™ books are created by a professional team of educators, reading specialists, and content developers around five essential components—phonemic awareness, phonics, vocabulary, text comprehension, and fluency—to assist young readers as they develop reading skills and strategies and increase their general knowledge. All books are written, reviewed, and leveled for guided reading, early reading intervention, and Accelerated Reader® programs for use in shared, guided, and independent reading and writing activities to support a balanced approach to literacy instruction. The SandCastle™ series has four levels that correspond to early literacy development. The levels help teachers and parents select appropriate books for young readers.

Emerging Readers
(no flags)

Beginning Readers
(1 flag)

Transitional Readers
(2 flags)

Fluent Readers
(3 flags)

These levels are meant only as a guide. All levels are subject to change.

We measure **liquid** by pouring it into a measuring cup. Lines on the measuring cup tell how much there is.

Words used to talk about measuring liquids:

**centimeter
inch
line
measuring cup
milliliter
ounce
teaspoon**

I put my on the so it will be level when I look at the lines on the cup.

In science class, I measure 100 milliliters of for an experiment. Millileters are one unit of measure used for liquids.

I measure eight ounces of juice to drink. Ounces are another unit of measure used for liquids.

I measure four ounces
of for my .

7

I measure two ounces

of syrup to pour over

my .

My backyard gauge shows that

one-half inch of rain fell.

Let's Be Kids and Measure Liquids!

Ingrid and Sid

have soup in a bowl.

Splitting it equally

is their goal.

They each set down

a measuring cup

and get ready to

divide the soup up.

Sid announces,
"Our cups measure
in ounces!"

Sid pours soup
into cup number one
and takes a look
to see what he's done.
Sid pours soup
into cup number two
and looks again closely
to get a good view.

When I look
at the lines,
I see Ingrid's
cup has more
than mine.

Ingrid uses a spoon
to even it out
until the soup is equal
beyond any doubt.
Ingrid and Sid
are two kids
who know how to
measure liquids.

Ingrid and I
let out a whoop
because we each have
eight ounces of soup!

15

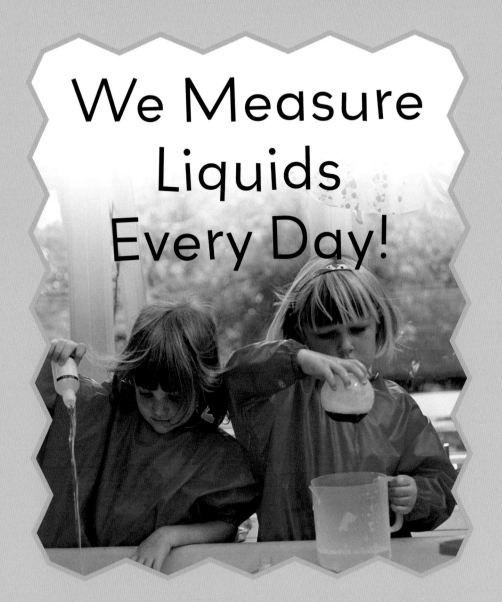

We Measure Liquids Every Day!

Haley measures water for a class project. She sets the measuring cup on the counter before she measures.

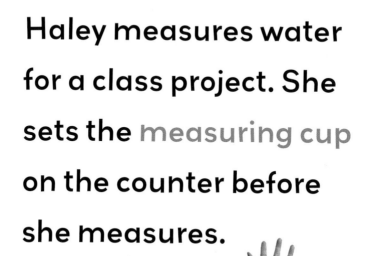

Haley knows the cup should be sitting level when she measures.

The rain gauge measures how much rain falls in Kaya's backyard. She looks at the rain gauge at eye level and reads the nearest line.

Kaya's rain gauge shows the measurement in both inches and centimeters.

Henry takes cough syrup to help him feel better. His mom measured it in the tiny measuring cup that came with it.

Liquid medicine can be measured in milliliters or teaspoons.

Matt's baby brother will drink 125 milliliters of formula. His mom measured the right amount for one meal.

What other liquids do you measure before you use them?

Glossary

formula – liquid food for babies.

milliliter – a unit of measurement in the metric system. There are 1,000 milliliters in a liter.

ounce – a unit of measurement in the U.S. customary system. There are eight ounces in a cup.

rain gauge – a tool used to measure how much rain has fallen.

teaspoon – a unit of measurement usually used for food or medicine.

whoop – a loud, happy shout.